WOMEN OVER
50
ARE BETTER BECAUSE...

Written By:
Herbert Kavet

Illustrated By:
Martin Riskin

Manufactured in the United States of America

30 29 28 27 26 25 24 23 22 21 20 19 18 17 16 15 14 13 12 11 10 9 8 7 6 5 4 3 2 1

Ivory Tower Publishing Co., Inc.
125 Walnut St., P.O. Box 9132, Watertown, MA 02272-9132
Telephone #: (617) 923-1111   Fax #: (617) 923-8839

WOMEN OVER 50 ARE BETTER BECAUSE...

They can finally afford all the things they no longer want.

WOMEN OVER 50 ARE BETTER BECAUSE...

They don't believe all the things men whisper in their ear.
They don't get terribly embarrassed by them either.

WOMEN OVER 50 ARE BETTER BECAUSE...

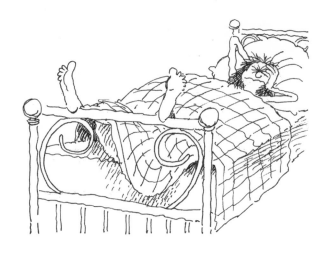

They know when they've had enough to drink and nothing
is worth that hangover the next day.

WOMEN OVER 50 ARE BETTER BECAUSE...

They have achieved a reasonable accommodation
with their exercise program.

WOMEN OVER 50 ARE BETTER BECAUSE...

They start dressing for comfort rather than blindly
following the latest styles.

WOMEN OVER 50 ARE BETTER BECAUSE...

They finally realize that their mother isn't the greatest cook in the world. At least she remembers that you hate cauliflower.

WOMEN OVER 50 ARE BETTER BECAUSE...

Fine establishments actually solicit them to carry their credit cards.

WOMEN OVER 50 ARE BETTER BECAUSE...

They can't be pressured into driving faster than they feel comfortable doing.

WOMEN
OVER
50
ARE BETTER
BECAUSE...

They replace the "Save The Whales" bumper sticker with "World's Greatest Mom".

**WOMEN
OVER
50
ARE BETTER
BECAUSE...**

They may have trouble with forgetting things but
they have their reminder systems down pat.

WOMEN OVER 50 ARE BETTER BECAUSE...

They are not afraid to include a few weirdos among their friends.

WOMEN OVER 50 ARE BETTER BECAUSE...

They have a favorite mechanic who is happy to help them out in an emergency.

WOMEN OVER 50 ARE BETTER BECAUSE...

They fantasize about going into business for themselves.

WOMEN OVER 50 ARE BETTER BECAUSE...

They don't care where their husbands go when they go out as long as they don't have to go with them.

WOMEN OVER 50 ARE BETTER BECAUSE...

They find themselves on virtually every junk mail list in the country. During the Christmas season they receive 43 full color catalogs every day.

WOMEN OVER 50 ARE BETTER BECAUSE...

Their eyes are as good as ever; it's just that their arms are growing shorter.

WOMEN OVER 50 ARE BETTER BECAUSE...

They know the proper pronunciation of at least three wines that they like and don't give a hoot about which goes well with what foods.

WOMEN OVER 50 ARE BETTER BECAUSE...

They don't pretend to be virgins.

WOMEN OVER 50 ARE BETTER BECAUSE...

They know exactly which foods are incompatible with their digestive systems.

**WOMEN
OVER
50
ARE BETTER
BECAUSE...**

They won't make you sleep in the middle
of their stuffed animal collection.

WOMEN OVER 50 ARE BETTER BECAUSE...

They will respect you in the morning.

WOMEN OVER 50 ARE BETTER BECAUSE...

They can eat a double-fudge chocolate sundae and not get any pimples, but they have to go to 3 aerobic classes to work it off—so they skip it anyway.

WOMEN OVER 50 ARE BETTER BECAUSE...

They can recognize and pronounce the names
of at least 3 French wines.

**WOMEN
OVER
50
ARE BETTER
BECAUSE...**

They can offer a critical analysis of every fad diet
to come along in the last 30 years.

WOMEN OVER 50 ARE BETTER BECAUSE...

The realize that no matter how many sit-ups and leg raises they do, they cannot recapture their 17-year-old figures.

They have a few favorite secret recipes that can get them through any crisis.

WOMEN OVER 50 ARE BETTER BECAUSE...

They actually look forward to dull evenings at home.

WOMEN OVER 50 ARE BETTER BECAUSE...

They start taking a serious interest in investment and savings plans.

WOMEN OVER 50 ARE BETTER BECAUSE...

Their years of expertise enable them to know exactly what is going wrong with their cars. Still, they can't get anyone competent to fix it.

**WOMEN
OVER
50
ARE BETTER
BECAUSE...**

They appreciate the advantages of control-top pantyhose.

WOMEN OVER 50 ARE BETTER BECAUSE...

They can afford an occasional splurge.

WOMEN OVER 50 ARE BETTER BECAUSE...

They can buy a car without soliciting advice from their father.

WOMEN OVER 50 ARE BETTER BECAUSE...

They are never too scared to enjoy sex.

WOMEN OVER 50 ARE BETTER BECAUSE...

They no longer apologize for gay or weird friends.

WOMEN OVER 50 ARE BETTER BECAUSE...

They can find something attractive in any 21-year-old guy.

**WOMEN
OVER
50
ARE BETTER
BECAUSE...**

They truly know the value of a good friend.

WOMEN OVER 50 ARE BETTER BECAUSE...

They can smoothly put down propositions from
the drunkest chauvinist.

WOMEN OVER 50 ARE BETTER BECAUSE...

They've tried every diet known to womankind, but no longer throw out their oversized clothes at the end of a successful one.

WOMEN OVER 50 ARE BETTER BECAUSE...

They have kids to help out with the real tough jobs.

WOMEN OVER 50 ARE BETTER BECAUSE...

They don't contemplate suicide at the end of an affair.

WOMEN OVER 50 ARE BETTER BECAUSE...

They realize their father was right when he said it was as easy to fall in love with a rich guy as a poor one.

WOMEN OVER 50 ARE BETTER BECAUSE...

They are wise enough to enjoy sports as a spectator rather than risk injuring themselves.

WOMEN OVER 50 ARE BETTER BECAUSE...

They know how to organize a truly great party.

WOMEN OVER 50 ARE BETTER BECAUSE...

They are smart enough to hire someone to do the cleaning.

WOMEN OVER 50 ARE BETTER BECAUSE...

They are willing to leave boring parties early.

They've stopped smoking, drink with moderation
and eat sensibly. Still, they always carry antacid pills.

WOMEN OVER 50 ARE BETTER BECAUSE...

They don't catch colds very often but hurt for a week after moving the refrigerator.

**WOMEN
OVER
50
ARE BETTER
BECAUSE...**

Men at the office actually solicit their advice.

WOMEN OVER 50 ARE BETTER BECAUSE...

They no longer sleep soundly through the night but can fall asleep instantly at any dull meeting.

WOMEN
OVER
50
ARE BETTER
BECAUSE...

Expletives don't embarrass them and they are able to use them at appropriate moments.

WOMEN OVER 50 ARE BETTER BECAUSE...

They know just what it takes to make their man feel good.

WOMEN OVER 50 ARE BETTER BECAUSE...

They finally stopped waiting for the baby fat to disappear.

WOMEN OVER 50 ARE BETTER BECAUSE...

They know how to start a car on fiercely cold mornings.

WOMEN OVER 50 ARE BETTER BECAUSE...

The kids are finally out of the house.

WOMEN
OVER
50
ARE BETTER
BECAUSE...

They know being alone is better than being
with someone they don't like.

**WOMEN
OVER
50
ARE BETTER
BECAUSE...**

They know their exact alcohol limits.

WOMEN OVER 50 ARE BETTER BECAUSE...

They don't care if their man has a night out with the boys while they stay home and sleep.

WOMEN OVER 50 ARE BETTER BECAUSE...

They know exactly what they like, and what they like costs a fortune.

WOMEN OVER 50 ARE BETTER BECAUSE...

They don't nag–they gently remind you.

**WOMEN
OVER
50
ARE BETTER
BECAUSE...**

They find obscene phone calls a mildly amusing form
of entertainment.

WOMEN OVER 50 ARE BETTER BECAUSE...

They have great liquor cabinets.

WOMEN OVER 50 ARE BETTER BECAUSE...

They can go to the movies alone on a Saturday night and not feel the least embarrassed.

WOMEN OVER 50 ARE BETTER BECAUSE...

They will let you watch football, basketball or any sport on TV and not be upset because you're ignoring them.

**WOMEN
OVER
50
ARE BETTER
BECAUSE...**

They can shop for a car with the acuteness of an
automotive engineer.

WOMEN OVER 50 ARE BETTER BECAUSE...

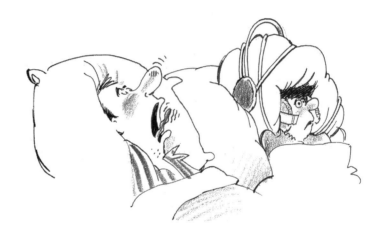

They can tune out even the worst snoring.

WOMEN OVER 50 ARE BETTER BECAUSE...

They don't believe all the ads for moisturizers and skin restorers, but they buy them anyway.

WOMEN OVER 50 ARE BETTER BECAUSE...

They finally realize that no one cares anymore about what they did in high school.

They are not afraid to redecorate.

WOMEN OVER 50 ARE BETTER BECAUSE...

They won't blush if you take them to an X-rated movie.

They are occasionally offered assistance from totally unexpected sources.

WOMEN OVER 50 ARE BETTER BECAUSE...

They start to hang around with new grandparents.
Of course, most are much older than they are.

WOMEN OVER 50 ARE BETTER BECAUSE...

They don't expect as much foreplay because they want to get to the heart of the matter.

WOMEN OVER 50 ARE BETTER BECAUSE...

They will be amused if you take them parking.

**WOMEN
OVER
50
ARE BETTER
BECAUSE...**

They can remember the punch line to at least 3 dirty jokes.

WOMEN OVER 50 ARE BETTER BECAUSE...

They are happy to hang out on the couch on Friday nights instead of going out.

WOMEN OVER 50 ARE BETTER BECAUSE...

They can see just fine if they squint a little during candlelight dinners.

WOMEN OVER
50
ARE BETTER
BECAUSE...

They have more womanly figures.

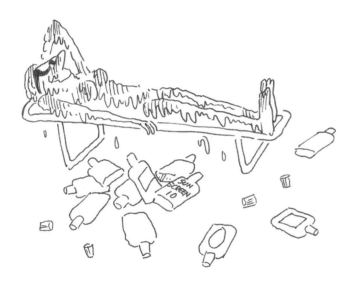

WOMEN OVER 50 ARE BETTER BECAUSE...

They can single-handedly support the entire sunscreen industry.

WOMEN OVER 50 ARE BETTER BECAUSE...

They live in a place where noisy parties, littering, sex fiends,
drug dealers and people crossing against the lights
are all frowned upon.

WOMEN OVER 50 ARE BETTER BECAUSE...

They don't fall to pieces if you see them without their makeup.

WOMEN OVER 50 ARE BETTER BECAUSE...

They are no longer very concerned about being "with it".

WOMEN OVER 50 ARE BETTER BECAUSE...

They have learned to live with pets.

WOMEN OVER 50 ARE BETTER BECAUSE...

They can usually find a "contact" to help them out with difficult situations.

WOMEN OVER 50 ARE BETTER BECAUSE...

They have great lingerie collections.

WOMEN OVER 50 ARE BETTER BECAUSE...

They know how to handle temporary lapses in performance.

WOMEN OVER 50 ARE BETTER BECAUSE...

Banks start to trust them.

WOMEN OVER 50 ARE BETTER BECAUSE...

They start to make some real contributions in their field.

WOMEN OVER 50 ARE BETTER BECAUSE...

They have a handle on all the latest fashions.

WOMEN OVER 50 ARE BETTER BECAUSE...

Their bookshelf is overflowing with "How To" and "Self Improvement" books that they don't bother to read.

WOMEN OVER 50 ARE BETTER BECAUSE...

You no longer have to give them birthday presents. They plot revenge on people who give them books like this one.

Other books we publish are available at many fine stores. If you can't find them, send directly to us. $7.00 postpaid

2400-How To Have Sex On Your Birthday. Finding a partner, special birthday sex positions, kinky sex on your birthday and much more.

2402-Confessions From The Bathroom. There are things in this book that happen to all of us that none of us ever talk about. The Gas Station Dump, for example, or the Corn Niblet Dump, the Porta Pottie Dump and more.

2403-The Good Bonking Guide. Bonking is a great new British term for doing "you know what". Covers bonking in the dark, bonking all night long, improving your bonking, and everything else you've ever wanted to know.

2407-40 Happens. When being out of prune juice ruins your whole day and you realize anyone with the energy to do it on a weeknight must be a sex maniac.

2408-30 Happens. When you take out a lifetime membership at your health club, and you still wonder when the baby fat will finally disappear.

2409-50 Happens. When you remember when "made in Japan" meant something that didn't work, and you can't remember what you went to the top of the stairs for.

2411-The Geriatric Sex Guide. It's not his mind that needs expanding; and you're in the mood now, but by the time you're naked, you won't be!

2412-Golf Shots. What excuses to use to play through first, ways to distract your opponent, and when and where a true golfer is willing to play.

2414-60 Happens. When your kids start to look middle-aged, when software is some kind of comfortable underwear, and when your hearing is perfect if everyone would just stop mumbling.

2416-The Absolutely Worst Fart Book. The First Date Fart, The Oh My God Don't Let Me Fart Now Fart, The Lovers' Fart, The Doctor's Exam Room Fart and many more.

2417-Women Over 30 Are Better Because... Their nightmares about exams are starting to fade and their handbags can sustain life for about a week with no outside support whatsoever.

2418-9 Months In The Sac. A humorous look at pregnancy through the eyes of the baby, such as: why do pregnant women have to go to the bathroom as soon as they get to the store, and why does baby start doing aerobics when it's time to sleep?

2419-Cucumbers Are Better Than Men Because... Cucumbers are always ready when you are and cucumbers will never hear "yes, yes" when you're saying "NO, NO."

2421-Honeymoon Guide. Every IMPORTANT thing to know about the honeymoon — from The Advantages Of Undressing With The Light On (it's slightly easier to undo a bra) to What Men Want Most (being allowed to sleep right afterwards without having to talk about love).

2422-Eat Yourself Healthy. Calories only add up if the food is consumed at a table. Snacking and stand up nibbling don't count. Green M&M's are full of the same vitamins found in broccoli and lots of other useful eating information your mother never told you.

2423-Is There Sex After 40? Your wife liked you better when the bulge above your waist used to be the bulge in your trousers. You think wife-swapping

means getting someone else to cook for you.

2424-Is There Sex After 50? Going to bed early just means a chance to catch up on your reading or watch a little extra t.v., and you find that you actually miss trying to make love quietly so as not to wake the children.

2425-Women Over 40 Are Better Because... Over 40 reasons why women over 40 really are better: They realize that no matter how many sit-ups and leg raises they do, they cannot recapture their 17-year-old figures—but they can find something attractive in any 21-year-old guy.

2426-Women Over 50 Are Better Because... More reasons why women over 50 are better: They will be amused if you take them parking, and they know that being alone is better than being with someone they don't like.

2427-You Know You're Over The Hill When... You tend to repeat yourself. All the stories of your youth have already bored most acquaintances several times over. Even worse, you've resigned to being slightly overweight after trying every diet that has come along in the last 15 years.

2428-Beer Is Better Than Women Because (Part II)... A beer doesn't get upset if you call it by the wrong name; and after several beers, you can roll over and go to sleep without having to talk about love.

2429-Married To A Computer. You're married to a computer if you fondle it daily, you keep in touch when you're travelling and you stare at it a lot without understanding it. You even eat most

meals with it. Truly advanced computers are indistinguishable from coke machines.

2430-Is There Sex After 30? By the time you're 30, parking isn't as much fun as it was in high school. He thinks foreplay means parading around nude in front of the mirror, holding his stomach in; and she has found that the quickest way to get rid of an unwanted date is to start talking about commitment.

2431-Happy Birthday You Old Fart! You're an Old Fart when you spend less and less time between visits to a toilet, your back goes out more than you do, you tend to refer to anyone under 40 as a "kid," and you leave programming the VCR to people under 25.

2432-Big Weenies. Why some people have big weenies while other people have teenie weenies; how to find big weenies in a strange town; rating a weenie; as well as the kinds of men who possess a putz, a prong, a schwanz, a member, a rod and a wang—and more!

2433-Games You Can Play With Your Pussy. Why everyone should have a pussy; how to give a pussy a bath (grease the sides of the tub so it won't be able to claw its way out); dealing with pussy hairs (shellac it so the hairs stay right where they belong); and everything else you ever wanted to know about pussies.

2434-Sex And Marriage. What wives want out of marriage (romance, respect and a Bloomingdale's Charge Card); what husbands want out of marriage (to be left alone when watching football games and to be allowed to go to sleep after sex).

Ivory Tower Publishing Co., Inc., 125 Walnut St., P.O. Box 9132, Watertown, MA 02272-9132   Tel: (617) 923-1111